It's All about the *Weddings*

Dr. Joseph A. Herr

ISBN 979-8-88832-796-8 (paperback)
ISBN 979-8-88832-798-2 (hardcover)
ISBN 979-8-88832-797-5 (digital)

Christian Faith Publishing
832 Park Avenue
Meadville, PA 16335
www.christianfaithpublishing.com

All biblical citations were taken from the New King James Version of the Holy Bible.

Printed in the United States of America

Preface

For the last several years, I have been on a mission to find these hidden secrets and teach them so that as many as possible understand the total meaning behind God's Word. I started an upper-room discussion at our two churches and invited everyone to come. Nothing was a sacred cow, too tough, or too sensitive. Everyone is invited regardless of where they attend church. These are extremely successful in both churches; in fact, we are getting people at both churches who will come to the upper room but not to our weekly worship services, which is all right in my mind. Many times, they will bring up questions and even challenge doctrine based on what they have learned in the past. I am dedicated to the *truth*, so *all* answers are from the Scripture.

This narrative is about my recent journey in the Word and God revealing the divine secret to me at 2:00 a.m. The Lord has blessed me in the past with hidden mysteries about the meaning of the Word. In most cases, they were very specific to scripture or topic. This mystery revealed at two o'clock in the morning in early June of 2022 was significantly different. It started with people questioning my belief concerning the rapture. I was hearing from the usual naysayers, but even others, some people whom I have admired and even followed some of their teachings, were now questioning the pretribulation rapture that I have firmly held. One pastor that has an audience that spans the globe changed his position to a teaching of "no rapture" but with no real evidence I could locate. I honestly don't mind when people disagree with me, except when they can't back it up with scripture. Then I had a theologian that I really admire who gave me a couple scriptures he said he found were problematic for the pretribulation rapture. Now I had something to work with; all I had to do was provide an answer to his question. I know without a shadow of a doubt that if I correctly interpret scripture, there is no scripture that should conflict with other scriptures. I am also confident that I can find the answer, if it exists. Everything has an answer if we dig and seek hard enough. I was searching but was not finding my answer; then all of a sudden, the revealing of the mystery appeared when I least expected it (somewhat like the rapture), and it totally not only explained the few scriptures that were being questioned, but it completely illuminated a lot of other scriptures throughout the *entire Bible*. It answered many of the questions, confusion, and even conflict that others were using to debate the truth or were struggling with. With running two churches, I usually do not have time to write anything that is more than a sermon length long. This divine secret has changed so much and allowed both of my congregations to better see many areas of the Bible like they had never imagined. I feel I was instructed to write it down so others can know. I hope it changes your spiritual life as much as it has changed some of my church families.

Before you start reading, God has blessed me continually by bringing me the experts I have needed to provide the information and understanding, when I have needed them. Praise God! Right at the beginning of my career, *God* introduced me to one of *His true generals, Brother Kenneth E. Hagin*. I have continued to follow *Brother Kenneth E. Hagin's* teachings, and he is, *without question*, the reason I am where I am today and know what I know. Getting in the Word has given me a love for the Jewish people and a desire to know all I can about Jewish culture and life throughout biblical times, but I do not claim to be an expert on Jewish culture. Several years ago, God put another great resource concerning the Jewish culture in my path, *Ray Vander Laan*, the founder of the *That the World Would Know* ministries. He has an amazing series of DVDs that are so full of information about Israel and its culture—*information that believers in the West normally have never heard*. Ray's DVDs are *invaluable* and should be in every pastor's library; they have provided me with much of what I needed to understand a lot of the *gold nuggets* that are hidden in the Word. Another resource is the documentary, "Before the Wrath," which was very helpful in validating my understanding of the Galilean wedding. Some of my knowledge has come from great authors like Rabbi Johnathan Cann and Rabbi Jason Sobel, personal relationships with other rabbis, and various other sources along with personal visits to Jerusalem. Just recently, God has guided me to a very special woman *Billye Brim*. I asked God why didn't I know about her before. God answered me, saying, *"You were not ready."* I've found that her *3BI Institute_offers a different level of knowledge and understanding of scripture and Jewish culture than I received from any university or seminary.* Two other awesome resources are books by Clarence Larkin, *Rightly Dividing the Word* and *Clarence Larkin Charts Collection*. I can almost guarantee that you will be amazed and blessed with both books.

I could have never understood the mystery God revealed to me without the knowledge, wisdom, and understanding I have received from these people, along with correctly interpreting the Word and much digging and seeking. I am greatly thankful to all of them. The *most important of all is God, who is always there* and has provided me with great insight. *None of what you are about to read is me, it is all Him*; I could never have come up with this—it was *all Him*.

Introduction

Like many who have abided in *His* Word (*in Him*), I have fallen in Love with our Lord. I am constantly trying to get closer and closer to Him in any way I can. I really enjoy it when someone says, "I never heard that before," or when they say, "I've *never* heard a pastor say that before." To me, it is God's affirmation that they are learning the mystery He has shown them. One area where many misinterpret scripture is on fearing God. I believe and teach that our fear must be a trembling, more than just a reverent fear; but it's important to understand that as our maturity increases and we become more like *agape*, the special love of God that our fear changes, it becomes what I call an addictive fear as we mature in our growth in Him. It's like whenever any addict loses the cause of their addiction, they go crazy with terrible fear, and they need their fix. Without it, they do not feel they can live. That is how I am with God. I love Him so much that if I am away from Him, I become fearful; it is still a trembling, frightful fear. I need Him and only Him. I *cherish my Father in heaven* and ask myself, How can I please *Him more*? He is my *addiction*, and I never want to *lose Him in any way*. That is why I spend the time I do studying extensively to know *Him* by immersing myself in His Word and examining every word. I don't have any special or secret tools. God has blessed me with the ability to attain a high level of education, a doctor of theology (DTh); however, I rarely advertise it. The letters behind a name do not define the person nor indicate their level of knowledge. I am still seeking more knowledge, wisdom, and understanding every day because it is so critical to understanding the whole picture. I've found that a lot of critical understanding comes from a different type of textbook. It is as He tells us to abide *in Him* so he will abide *in* us. There is a secret code that opens many of the doors of understanding; it is *the culture in which Jesus lived and how He used this in His communication with the disciples.* The more we learn this, the more we can understand not only the *words used* but also *the message* he was giving to the disciples. This has been a wonderful journey, and I know I still have a long way to go. Every turn I make, I find a new divine secret that just illuminates another piece.

God speaks of many mysteries; all of them are in the New Testament, and twenty-one out of twenty-seven are in the Epistles written specifically to the body of Christ (the bride). Mystery in Greek is *mustĕriŏn* Strong's 3466, which states the definition as "a secret or mystery (through the idea of *silence* imposed by *initiation* into religious rites)"; it is a "*divine secret.*" Most of these divine secrets are to the body of Christ because God purposely hid them until the time was right (Daniel 12:4). Some of the secrets were specific to a culture of which the Gentiles and at times even some Jews were unaware. Therefore, it is so very important that when we are seeking and searching for the truth, we do it properly. I learned several years ago to answer some basic questions to accurately understand scripture and capture the complete message. Those simple questions are

1. Who is the author?
2. Who is the audience?
3. What is the message the author is trying to convey?
4. What is the setting at the time?
5. Is the author using language from something common in their life that helps them understand their message?

Every time I've encountered confusion with the Scripture, a misunderstanding, or someone saying a certain scripture is in conflict with others, it usually is because one of the above cardinal *rules of interpretation* has been violated. I have also seen where so many are teaching things that are inappropriate or even apostate because they have misinterpreted or violated one of the above and are applying a message given to and about a certain audience and not intended for them. Many times, this may turn out okay because the advice is good for everyone, but often it is very specific. If you ever find conflict in the Word or confusion, I believe if you go back and closely look, you probably have missed one of the above. When teaching this, often my students are confused, so let me briefly explain. Too many treat the Bible as two separate books; this causes much confusion. Also, Sister Billye Brim has a little booklet entitled *Rightly Defining the Word*. This describes the process in very simple-to-understand language, which is important to *enable* you to correctly understand the *Word*, the prophecies, and the different covenants and promises that are directed to a specific group, and *if* they apply to you.

Like many of you, I search for the truth constantly, even after finding the truth if someone provides a reasonable argument. I study and discern the argument to determine if it contains any credibility. God has always clarified any confusion created by what seemed once to be scripture in conflict with the *truth*. Caution, there are still truths that we don't know or understand because God hasn't revealed them yet and may not reveal them until He comes again.

It is important that the body of Christ is unified in faith. Ephesians 4:13 states, "Till we all come to the unity of the faith and of the knowledge of the Son of God, to a perfect man, to the measure of the stature of the fullness of Christ." Wow, as members of the body of Christ, each of us is building ourselves up in our knowledge of the *Word*, Jesus Christ, and truly becoming as *one* in our faith in *Him* so that we truly become one *in Him* and abide *in Him* and *He in us*.

Satan's Deceptions

Satan is working today just the same as he did when he talked with Eve. Then the serpent said to the woman, "You will not surely die. For God knows that in the day you eat of it your eyes will be opened, and you will be like God, knowing good and evil" (Genesis 3:4–5). Many are sincerely looking for the truth, but Satan's cunning is showing them scripture out of context, or in many cases, he is confusing the way they divide the Word or using our lack of understanding of specifics of the Galilean life and culture that illuminated many of Jesus's conversations.

From my spiritual infancy, it seems that there are arguments within the body of Christ about the nature, the timing, and even the validity of God's *Word*. The *truth* in many cases has been overtaken by man's doctrine, emotions, or in many cases the altering of the message to make it more appealing or even easy so as not to burden anyone.

Today we are experiencing exactly what scripture warns us; the wolves in sheep's clothing have infiltrated the buildings of the church, and most church buildings are just like the churches Jesus addressed in Revelation. They have succumbed to the exact things that Jesus said they had to *overcome*. They are beautiful on the outside but a graveyard on the inside. Like the churches in Revelation, they are unaware that anything is wrong.

For all who are looking to overcome the evils of the world, *our awesome God* has provided hidden *sacred secrets* to help us get through the turmoil of confusion and have unity. Sometimes the secrets are there because if *all* we understand is the definition of the words used in the Scripture, we miss so much of what God intended for us to know, which causes us to *miss* some of the special things *God* has hidden in *His* beautiful narrative. As a result, we do not have the full knowledge of the lessons Christ has given to us, which allows for confusion and even conflict in understanding scripture that ultimately fosters disunity. In the first chapter of Ephesians, Paul prays for all the saints, those who are faithful in Jesus Christ, that is you and me, in verses 17–21. He prays

> That the God of our Lord Jesus Christ, the Father of glory, may give to you the spirit of wisdom and revelation in the knowledge of Him, the eyes of your understanding being enlightened; that you may know what is the hope of His calling, what are the riches of the glory of His inheritance in the saints, and what is the exceeding greatness of His power toward us who believe, according to the working of His mighty power which He worked in Christ when He raised Him from the dead and seated Him at His right hand in the heavenly places, far above all principality and power and might and dominion, and every name that is named, not only in this age but also in that which is to come.

Ever since He revealed the great divine secret to me, my eyes have been enlightened, I have gained a new view of His inheritance, and He has opened the entire Bible up in such a way that I see Him in a more glorious and intimate way than ever before. I thought I knew Him and who I was in Him, but I was only scratching the surface. Since His revealing, it seems that I cannot read any scripture in the old covenant or the new without seeing and experiencing a deeper relationship than before (and before I didn't think there was anything closer and deeper). I pray as you read my account that you too will experience a closeness and a deeper relationship than you thought possible.

A Large Part of Knowing Christ Is the Culture

Knowing *His culture* and *how He used it in His messages* is where we find the clues to many of the answers to the *divine secrets*.

God illuminates scripture by using the normal things in the Jewish everyday life. The more I learn, the more *He* has clarified *His Word* for me. Things we normally would not even think could hold hidden secrets, like the design of the tabernacle. That detail is for another book, but the summary is that the design of the tabernacle helps us understand two areas that are so critical.

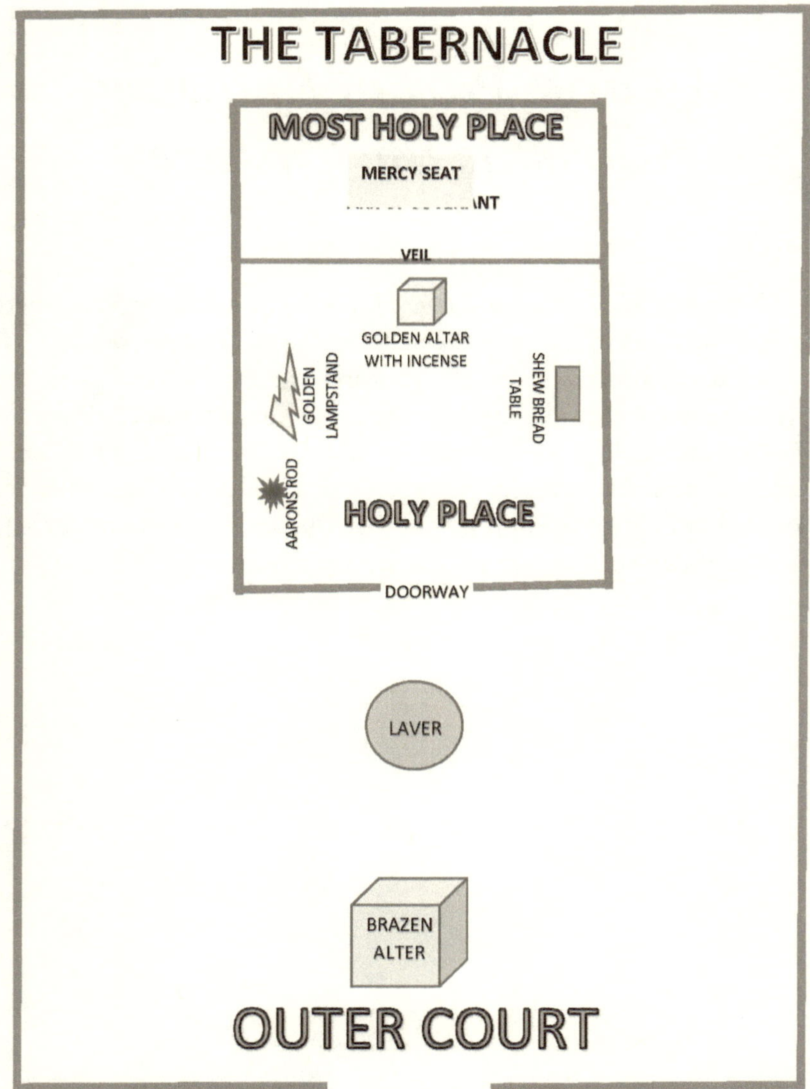

ORGANIZED AS A TRIUNE JUST LIKE OUR TRIUNE GOD

1. There is so much confusion about the soul and spirit and how they work together. The picture of the tabernacle provides a simple snapshot. The tabernacle is made up of three specific areas that relate to the body, soul, and spirit of man. The courtyard is the body, the holy place is the soul, and the most holy place is the spirit. In the tabernacle, one cannot go from the courtyard to the most holy place; you must go through the holy place to get to the most holy place. It is the same in the Trinity of Man. Our outer courtyard, our body, is where all our senses reside, our emotions, and our fleshly likes and dislikes. Our soul is where our natural imagination, conscience, memory, reason, and affections all reside. Our spirit is the immortal spirit of *God* if we are truly following *Him*—it is where *He* resides; it is where true faith, hope, love, reverence, prayer, and worship comes from; and it is where our relationship with *Him* becomes *one*. Just like in the tabernacle, we cannot communicate anything directly from our body to our spirit; it must go through our physical soul first. This means that our physical soul must believe and trust before our spirit can.

2. God's divine template for man's redemption and spiritual transformation is represented through every aspect of the tabernacle. We will just cover the high-level points.

    a) The outer door is the only way, which symbolizes Jesus as "*the way*" (John 14:6).

    b) Once through the *way*, we encounter a brazen altar that represents our Lord Jesus's suffering on the cross where He bore the penalty for our sin.

    Surely our griefs He Himself bore, and our sorrows He carried; Yet we ourselves esteemed Him stricken, smitten of God, and afflicted. But He was pierced through for our transgressions, He was crushed for our iniquities; The chastening for our well-being fell upon Him, And by His scourging we are healed. All of us like sheep have

gone astray, each of us has turned to his own way;
But the LORD has caused the iniquity of us all to
fall on Him. (Isaiah 53:4–6)

c) The laver represents our water baptism.
d) Then we enter the inner door to the holy place; this
    is where we become as Paul describes in 2 Corinthians
    3:18, "But we all, with unveiled face, beholding as in
    a mirror the glory of the Lord, are being transformed
    into the same image from glory to glory, just as by the
    Spirit of the Lord." This is the door we open to have
    intimacy and fellowship with God.
e) The seven-branched *candlestand* is symbolic of the
    light of Jesus Christ. We need His light to guide us to
    the truth.
f) The table of shewbread represents the bread from
    heaven. Jesus is the bread from heaven and sustains
    all life; if we eat of *His bread*, we will have eternal life.

Then Jesus said to them, "Most assuredly,
I say to you, Moses did not give you the bread
from heaven, but My Father gives you the true
bread from heaven. For the bread of God is He
who comes down from heaven and gives life to
the world." Then they said to Him, "Lord, give
us this bread always." And Jesus said to them, "I
am the bread of life. He who comes to Me shall
never hunger, and he who believes in Me shall
never thirst." (John 6:32–35)

g) Aaron's rod was a symbol of authority, and because it
    budded (produced fruit), it was *a supernatural sign*,
    showing that God was bringing life into a dead piece
    of wood, just like He brings life into us even when we
    are completely dead in sin.

h)   The golden altar with incense was a place for all saints to come and pray, and the incense carried the sweet aroma of the prayers up to *God.* Because Jesus shed *His blood* on the altar for us, we now have access to *Him* through our prayer.

And whatever you ask in My name, that I will do, that the Father may be glorified in the Son. If you ask anything in My name, I will do it. (John 14:13–14)

i)   The holy of holies was the place that represents the most intimate of relationships with God. This is our final destiny, where we will spend eternity; if we stay the course and finish the race as Paul tells us, when we reach it, we then abide in the Shechinah glory, and He abides in us. The Shechinah glory is part of us—hallelujah.

Just a couple more examples of ancient Jewish culture that help explain different scriptures:

I.   A *ceremony* called Kezazah (cutting off) was used for prodigal sons who lost their inheritance to a Gentile. You see it was *not uncommon* (as many think and teach) to have a prodigal son leave home with his inheritance and go to a Gentile nation and lose everything, then return home with nothing. When he came back, there are varied descriptions of the actual ceremony, but the end is always the same—if the townspeople see him before the father and get him, they will surround him and chant, and at the end of the chant, they will throw a clay pot to the ground, breaking it in pieces. This symbolizes the broken relationship that now existed between the community and this sinner. The result is that this man is now permanently separated and exiled away from his family, his community, and his faith.

When we know this, it is easy to understand the extreme urgency that the father gets to his son *before* the townspeople, an urgency where the father did not care if he sinned or embarrassed himself greatly by showing the skin of his body. If he didn't get to his son before any of the townspeople, his son would be exiled from the community and his family *forever*.

II. In the story of Jesus and the adulterous woman, the Western world is trying to determine what Jesus is writing in the dirt. But to many Jews, they will say He is pronouncing a curse on them through Jeremiah 17:13,

> O LORD, the hope of Israel, all who forsake You shall be ashamed. Those who depart from Me Shall be written in the earth, because they have forsaken the LORD, The fountain of living waters.

The Pharisees knew that this verse is what Jesus was pointing to and that Jesus was cursing them because they had departed from the *Word*.

III. Understanding the life in the mountain deserts reveals several messages of life and death that Jesus referred to often in His lessons, which the Jews understood immediately, but the urgency is often missed by the Western world.

    a) The wadi is a channel worn through the rocky mountains, a result of rain that may fall many miles away. Much of the mountainous area receives no rain at all, but when the rain comes possibly fifty miles away, it becomes a raging flood through the mountains.

    b) The story of building on a solid foundation.

> Everyone then who hears these words of mine and does them will be like a wise man who built his house on the rock. And the rain fell, and the floods came, and the winds blew and beat

on that house, but it did not fall, because it had been founded on the rock. And everyone who hears these words of mine and does not do them will be like a foolish man who built his house on the sand. And the rain fell, and the floods came, and the winds blew and beat against that house, and it fell, and great was the fall of it. (Matthew 7:24–27)

Jesus was referring directly to the wadis. We know this because in this area, the wadi will flood after rain and wash everything away. It is deadly; often the largest number of lives lost in a year is due to the wadi floods because they come upon the shepherds so quickly. At the end of the wadi is a deposit of mostly sand where you would never want to build. But all around is solid rock safe to build on. The Israelites would have taken this teaching and understood immediately the life-and-death decision Jesus was talking about in this lesson.

c)   When Jesus talks about leaving the ninety-nine for the one, the Israelites would have also immediately understood the importance Jesus was placing on His lost sheep. The sheep would often wander away when they were thirsty, and the best place to find them was in the wadi because there were always pools of standing water (Psalm 23) where they would smell the water and go to quench their thirst. However, this is an extremely dangerous place for both the sheep and the shepherd. *But* the shepherd would always go to save that one sheep, risking his life for the one. So again, Jesus's lesson is heard by the Israelites in a life-and-death manner. They know the intimacy Jesus is telling them of *His love* for them, in a way that others could not know. The shepherd knows just how important the life of one sheep is and celebrates when the lost one is found, just as Jesus says that all in heaven rejoice when a lost soul is found.

    d)   The Israelites easily associate the danger the shepherd experiences for the sheep to the life Jesus has lived for mankind, plus they understand *His love* for us in a much more intimate way because He associates it directly with the dangers in the physical life they live daily.

IV.   The secrets in the desert illustrates God's promises being for *sustenance*, not *excess*.

    a)   The manna and quail in the desert were always just enough to last the day; if they took more than they needed, it would spoil.

    b)   The shade trees in the desert were trees we in the Western world would *never* sit under to seek relief from the sun. Their branches were sparse and provided little shade; but the Israelites knew when the sun was intense, they could sit under one of these trees, and it would provide enough protection from the sun to allow them to sustain life. Not comfortably, but they still lived.

V.   When my wife and I were in Jerusalem, we visited the mountains where the shepherds still feed their sheep. It is a very dramatic picture. You can see lines as if they were drawn horizontally across the mountainside. These are referred to as the straight and narrow paths. The sheep would follow the shepherds' call (the shepherds were young girls singing when we were there), and as long as the sheep stayed on the straight and narrow, they would find enough food to keep them alive. If they got off the straight and narrow, they would die. Even though they receive no rainfall, along the straight and narrow paths there are groups of stones where dew collects and allows maybe a half dozen blades of grass to grow; some refer to these few blades of grass as "green pastures." So you see how the people of the time would have known exactly what Jesus meant when he talked about the straight and narrow, and that it was a matter of life and death. This also provides a greater understanding of the great Psalm 23.

These are just a small tease of the secrets that lie there in the culture and understanding of the Jewish life in the day of Jesus that makes *His Word* come alive and shows how the disciples were able to understand things that had much greater meaning than the words being said.

Much of this is *critical* in our walk with Jesus because it is important to *God* that the body of Christ *is united in faith*. Knowing the secrets embedded in the culture like the Galilean wedding will clarify the understanding and enable the body to be unified as God desires. The following scriptures emphasize unity in the body: 1 Corinthians 1:10, 2 Corinthians 13:11, Philippians 2:2, Ephesians 4:13, and John 17:23. Learning the culture and specific details of the habits and social tradition and the ways of the day will help us all understand those *special mysteries (sacred secrets) that Jesus has hidden just for us to find. They are our treasures.*

The Divine Secret Exposed

There are a couple of very specific things I had been searching for the answers to. Little did I know that my whole belief system would be changed by the revealing of one of God's mysteries (divine secrets). The interesting thing, as you will notice, is the timing of the revealing. One night, the Lord woke me at 2:00 a.m. and flooded my mind with verses that many argue cause confusion. One was a verse a good friend of mine, one of the greatest theologians I know would tell me many times, "This verse is problematic for the rapture. God showed me that my confusion was due to listening to other experts rather than searching for myself. He cleared the confusion almost immediately, and it was almost as if He yelled, '*It's all about the wedding*.'"

I knew that the disciples did not have the New Testament to guide them because they were writing the New Testament, so how did they understand what Jesus was saying to them? When God said, "*It's all about the wedding*," bells went off in my head (not wedding bells), and it was like He slapped me—how could you not have seen this? I can now look and see that God used the wedding theme throughout the Old and New Testaments and specifically the Galilean wedding in the New Testament to communicate special messages that the disciples would pick up immediately! I became a little giddy and could not contain my excitement. I remember just *immediately* seeing different parts of the Bible and saying of course this is what he was saying.

The Galilean wedding was different from others. As I recalled the betrothal, wedding process, and wedding feast, *everything* just fell into place, not only with the rapture but with the book of Revelation and much more in the Bible. I started to see the wedding in areas of the Bible I never even thought about being associated with a wedding, and then *wow*, it was like God just opened new things everywhere I looked. I took all the parts of the Galilean wedding that I was familiar with and used my learning from *Rightly Dividing the Word*; the questions I had and all the verses that I was told were problematic, and the confusion that others were declaring became perfectly ordered. The answer was obvious for *Christ's redemption plan for man*, and while I thought I had a good understanding of the great book of Revelation, I now see it with clarity things that I never saw before. Before there was always a scripture or part of the book of Revelation that seemed to be in conflict with other scriptures, now I clearly see the blessing that is promised when we read, hear, and keep the knowledge of that book. I was floating on cloud nine, and God then put in my head, *Go write this down so you don't forget*. He knows that I forget what I said two minutes ago. I had been awake for almost two hours with all this flooding my mind, so at 4:00 a.m., I started the outline of what I had heard. I have shared the mystery God revealed to me with my two congregations, and with some close pastor friends and for all, so far, things they have always questioned and were afraid to mention have been suddenly illuminated. One area that really shocked me was the celebration of Communion. I have always been taught that Communion was about the remembrance of Jesus Christ and the renewal of the new covenant (our marriage vows), but I never associated the entire betrothal. Now the celebration is complete, and my churches clearly see and feel how precious and important that ordinance is. Every time it is celebrated, there is true worship and praise, and it is spirit filled throughout the entire service. Communion has almost become a complete service; it is amazing and so exhilarating, as Paul says in 1 Corinthians 11:17–29, we can now truly remember *Him* and celebrate *His* life, *His* example of living to follow, *His* sacrificed *body* for *His body*, the church, and the renewal of the new covenant so that *all* can remember it in the short wait until He comes again. Oh hallelujah, hallelujah, and hallelujah.

This is why I now feel that He wanted me to write this down to share it with all in this small booklet.

God's Purpose for Creation

The Bible is the history of *the greatest love* narrative ever recorded. Even though we treat the Bible as two distinct and different narratives, it is not; it is one narrative from Genesis through Revelation that is about two very important covenants. Too many try to take a microscope to the book and highlight the individual events before understanding the universal scenario.

From the very beginning, *God had one motive for all creation.* Many say that His motivation was to have a relationship; unfortunately, we do such an injustice to God's intent when we say He wants a relationship with us. No, brothers and sisters, from the very beginning, God wanted much more than just a relationship. He has wanted something much more intimate, much closer, and much greater than a relationship; He wants and needs a very *special* relationship. He wants a *real family—His real family with a bride and children.* His desire the entire time has been to have a true *godly family*, where He would have *that special intimacy* that only a family can bring. That is why the entire Word of God is designed around two very specific weddings (God the Father's wedding with the Jewish nation and the body of Christ's wedding to *the Lamb*). It is why God talks in detail about the relationships within a godly family, between husband and wife, children and parents, and God and family. It is also the reason that God *hates divorce* (Malachi 2:16).

God has designed the family structure *as it is in heaven.* The instructions He provides for us are meant for us to know what He *expects* and the perfection that He will have in heaven. Our time on earth is a time of probation, testing, and preparation, for when we as the body of Christ become His bride, individually each of us enters into *the family of God.* (Appendix A)

THE SPIRITUAL MYSTERY OF 7 DAYS

7 DAYS OF CREATION *DAY = 24 HOURS* 6 DAYS THEN DAY OF REST	7 DAYS FOR MANS REDEMPTION DAY = 1000 YEARS (SEE BELOW)	7 DAYS OF TRIBULATION DAY = 1 WEEK DANIEL'S 70 WEEKS JACOBS TROUBLE

7 TEARS = SHEMITAH CYCLE; ***THE SHEMITAH YEAR*** = A TIME FOR REST AND REJUVENATION

7 SHEMITAH CYCLES = *JUBILEE YEAR* A GLORIOUS TIME OF FREEDOM AND FORGIVENESS
(SLAVES FREED AND ALL DEBTS FORGIVEN)

7 DAYS GOD APPOINTED AS ***HIS DAYS*** REPRESENTING ***THE REDEEMING OF MAN*** (APPENDIX B)

PASSOVER *JESUS* *DEATH*	UNLEAVEN BREAD *JESUS'* *VICTORY* *OVER SIN &* *DEATH*	FIRST FRUITS *JESUS'* *RESSURECTION*	PENTECOST *BIRTH OF* *CHURCH* *WITH HOLY* *SPIRIT*	TRUMPETS *THE* *RAPTURE*	ATONEMENT OF THE JEWS THE TRIBULATION	TABERNACLE *MILLENIUM*

7 DAYS FOR REDEMTION OF MAN (A DAY IS AS A THOUSAND YEARS 2 PETER 3:8)

2 THOUSAND YEARS THE AGE OF IGNORANCE	2 THOUSAND YEARS THE AGE OF LAW	JESUS COMES	2 THOUSAND YEARS AGE OF GRACE	7 THOUSANDTH YEAR DAY OF REST THE MILLENIUM

There is a very special secret in the structure of *all* God's creation. It is in the numbers. One number that is important for *time* is the number 7; it represents *the idea of wholeness and perfection.* The seven days of creation ended with a perfect completion with a day of rest. With the fall of Adam and Eve, we also see that the redemption of man will require seven—seven days of one thousand years each (seven thousand years) to correct the damage done in the garden. I point this out so that you can see that God illuminates a lot of His Word with the numbers He uses. (See chart "The Spiritual Mystery of Seven Days")

Now for the number that is important for *His family.* It is the number 3. God created us in *His image and likeness.* We know that when Adam sinned, mankind lost some of that image because once we are born again, we are told that we are being *transformed into his image.* In 2 Corinthians 3:18 states, "But we all, with unveiled face, beholding as in a mirror the glory of the Lord, are being transformed into the same image from glory to glory, just as by the Spirit of the Lord." This transformation is what is required for us to get through our probation and testing period. There is, however, some of His likeness that all mankind still has; it is the very nature of our being. God is a Triune Godhead, and He created us in a similar pattern. The Godhead is the Father, Son, and Holy Spirit. He created mankind's body, soul, and spirit. If you think about it, our body is what everyone sees when they look at us—just like Jesus is what everyone sees, our soul is what guides us with our feelings and conscience, just like the Holy Spirit is the guide, and our spirit is something that is invisible, but it is our true *life* that is God the Father. The number 3 means divine fullness and completion, so the more I look around, I see the number 3 in all the *life* that *God* has created.

THE TRIUNE NATURE OF MAN

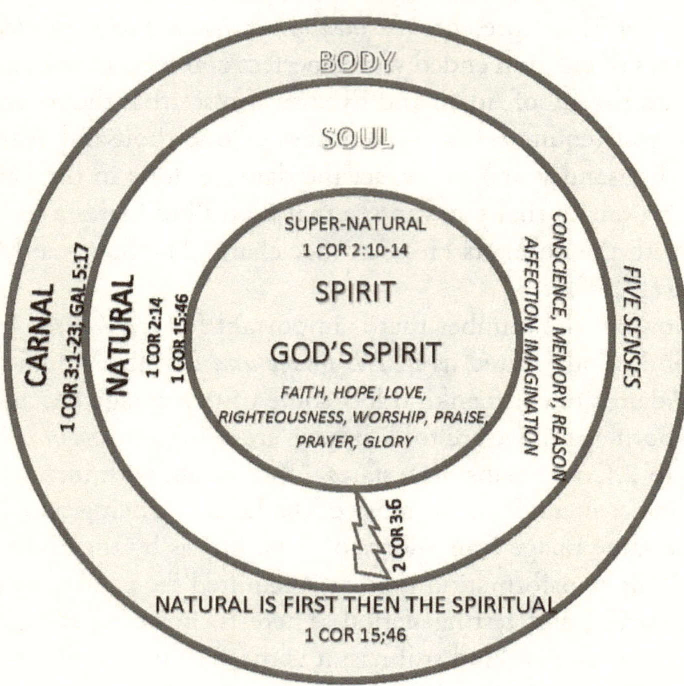

God's plan from the beginning was to have *his own family*, the true family of God, God with His bride and their children. The family of God in the Abrahamic covenant is the following:

Again, we see the number 3.

    a)   The *husband* is God the Father.
    b)   The *bride* is the nation of Israel.
    c)   The *children* are each member of the nation of Israel. This is not every Israelite. Romans 9:6–8 says, "For they are not all Israel which are of Israel; neither because they are the seed of Abraham are they all children…but the children of promise are counted for the seed."

d)   It *is* all who have faith and follow God's Word (Israelite and Gentile). Galatians 3:7 says, "Know ye therefore that they which are of faith, the same are the children of Abraham."

WORD OF GOD AND THE WEDDING

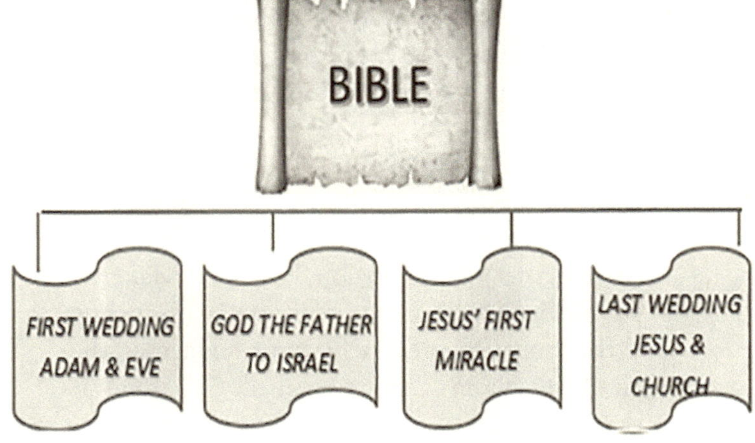

The family starts with the wedding, and when we look closely, we see the wedding and God's family throughout the whole Word of God. In fact, we know we can tell the end from the beginning (Isaiah 46:10), and we always have the natural first then the spiritual (1 Corinthians 15:16). The Bible starts with *the physical* wedding of man and woman and ends with *the spiritual* wedding of the Lamb of God to the body of Christ.

Some of the *highlights* in the Old Testament are these:

- Once everything else is created for man, the Bible begins man's journey with the first wedding of Adam and Eve—their purpose was to become one flesh as man and wife.
- After man's fall, we needed another covenant. The second marriage is with the Abrahamic covenant. This was the wedding vows between God the Father and the Jewish nation.

    This was an unconditional covenant established for an everlasting commitment between God and the Jewish Nation For your Maker is your husband, the Lord of hosts is his name; and the Holy One of Israel is your Redeemer, the God of the whole earth he is called. (Isaiah 54:5)

- Most of the Old Testament is describing *God the Father's* marriage troubles and *His* bride's unfaithfulness, constant complaining, and infidelity, even when the Shechinah glory was in their presence day and night, even after they would see his wrath (three thousand were killed when Moses came down the mountain with the Ten Commandments, and they had built the golden calf). Over and over God would correct them, and they would within a short time turn back to disobedience and idolatry.
- The children of God (the individual people of Israel) couldn't help themselves; they were in constant rebellion because they refused to treat God as their Father and rely on *Him* and *trust Him*. Their faith changed daily, like many today.
- The entire book of Hosea is a true story about the prophet Hosea, but it is also a true story of God the Father's turbulent wedding with the Jewish nation. They were constantly

committing adultery, even when God was right in their midst as a cloud by day and fire by night. But God took them back every time.

> And in that day, declares the LORD, you will call me "My Husband," and no longer will you call me "My Baal." For I will remove the names of the Baals from her mouth, and they shall be remembered by name no more. And I will make for them a covenant on that day with the beasts of the field, the birds of the heavens, and the creeping things of the ground. And I will abolish the bow, the sword, and war from the land, and I will make you lie down in safety. And I will betroth you to me forever. I will betroth you to me in righteousness and in justice, in steadfast love and in mercy. I will betroth you to me in faithfulness. And you shall know the LORD. (Hosea 2:16–20)

- After the miraculous freeing from Egypt, God attempted to fulfill His wedding vows by leading His bride into their promised land, but again they did not believe. So He forced them to wander in the desert for forty years until the unbelieving generation would pass away.
- Then after taking care of His bride for three hundred years since they were freed from Egypt, providing for them in every way, giving them leaders like Moses, Joshua, and all the judges, they wanted to be like other nations and have a *king*. They rejected God as their protector, king, and husband, relying on themselves instead of their husband. This was not what God wanted and really hurt. Of course, this is exactly what man has done and continues to do since the dawn of time; they rely on themselves and not their Creator. Isaiah 9 is a complete chapter on the curse that comes on man for trying to do things without God.

- All the prophets in the Old Testament cried out to the people to return to God and repent so they could remain His bride.

In the New Testament, the new covenant is the wedding vows for these:

1. The husband—Jesus Christ
2. The bride—The body of Christ, made up of all those who truly follow Jesus as He said in Matthew 16:24: Then Jesus said to His disciples, "If anyone desires to come after Me, let him deny himself, and take up his cross, and follow Me." Then in Matthew 10:38, "And he who does not take his cross and follow after Me is not worthy of Me."
3. The children—Each believer.
    - In the New Testament, Jesus's first miracle is where the Galilean wedding is first introduced. This is critical because this is where Jesus starts showing the pattern for communicating with the disciples throughout His ministry.

THE GALILEAN BETROTHAL	JESUS' LAST SUPPER A "COMMON-UNION"
Bride bought with a price	Bride of jesus bought with a price
***Time of remembrance for long separation	***Time of remembrance for long separation
Groom says his vows then offers bride the cup of wine	Jesus prays to the father *John 17* all the promises for the bride then offers bride the cup of wine
Bride agrees to the grooms vows by accepting the cup and drinking the wine	We agree to Jesus' vows by Accepting the cup and drinking the wine
Bride's vow to love, obey, & follow groom	We renew our vow to love, obey, & follow our groom JESUS
Here they were legally married (can be divorced) *Matthew 1:19*	We are legally married (*can be divorced if not ready upon his return*) *Matthew 24:32-51*
The groom and the bride will not drink from the fruit of the vine, until they drink it in the father's house, *at the weeding feast.*	Jesus says "I shall not drink from the fruit of the vine, until I drink it with you, in my Father's Kingdom." *(at the wedding feast)* *Matthew 26:29*
Groom says to bride "I go to prepare a room for you at my father's house"	Jesus says to bride *"I go to prepare a room for you at my father's house"* *John 14:2b*
The bride knows this is the grooms promise to return no matter how long *over 1 year*	We know this is Jesus' promise to return no matter how long ***over 2000 years John 14:3***

*** *Bread and wine used as a blessing for all covenants since Genesis 14. Jesus used bread for remembrance like the groom offered his bride bread for remembrance. The groom secretly provided gifts during the separation. Jesus provides us gifts through the Holy Spirit and Communion with Him.*

-   The Last Supper—The celebration of the Last Supper is misunderstood by many. When we put it into the context of the Galilean wedding, we see clearly that this is a time that Jesus is using bread and wine just like the groom and bride did at the betrothal. It is a time for remembrance the bride and groom will be apart for a very long time, so the bride especially needs to remember the Groom, everything He has done, His love, His sacrifices, and what their life together will be like when He returns. It is also a time to say or renew the wedding vows to show commitment and again to remember the precious promises. This is a time to remember Jesus the Groom for His life, His example He left us, His broken body, and the greatest sacrifice ever for His bride and a time for us as His bride constantly renews our wedding vows. Before supper had ended, Jesus really sealed the fact that He was referring to the Galilean wedding process. Every time we remember *Him* and renew our wedding vows, *He remembers us*! After the vows and right before the Groom would leave His bride, He would say, "I go now to build a room for you at my Father's house." The bride knew that Him saying that was a promise that He would return no matter how long it took to take her up to His Father's house. This puts a completely new meaning and an urgency on celebrating Communion. (See Appendix B)

Even at His death on the cross, the people with one accord accepted a natural man Barabbas. Some manuscripts call him Jesus Barabbas, which means Jesus, Son of the Father; if those scriptures are accurate, it puts a completely different twist on the encounter with Barabbas. Even if it is not accurate, this encounter affords every believer an awesome parallel to every believer's walk. Every one of us stands guilty before God, deserving death. But because of *His grace* and nothing we could *ever* do, through no influence, we could ever offer Jesus was chosen to die for us. He, being innocent, received the punishment we deserved. He did this because it is exactly what a godly husband is obligated to do through *His agape* (the special love of God). The people's rejection of Jesus and their acceptance of Barabbas were really a rejection of His wedding vows.

- Jesus's death on the cross is another example of His extreme *love* for all of us. Just a day after the Last Supper where He declared His wedding vows and where He told them, "I go now to prepare a room for you at my Father's house," like the Galilean groom says right before He leaves the bride for an *"extended period."* This is His promise to His bride—no matter how long the separation, to come back and *take her up to His Father's house.* Therefore, the disciples knew this was *Jesus's promise*, to come back and get them no matter how long it took. Unfortunately, the people's reaction demonstrated their lack of faith and trust, including (at least temporally) His closest disciples. In every account of His death, we see that *all* the disciples except one (John) abandoned Him and stayed in hiding until the day of Pentecost—a perfect example of how weak the flesh was. The only solidarity shown was with the women who always followed Him. What a great tribute Jesus shares about women at a time when they were truly second-class citizens at best. Need a second book to show how much God honored women and will honor them in His kingdom.
- His resurrection and assumption into heaven are representative of the groom leaving the bride alone for a long period.
- While He is gone, the bride must take care of all the wedding details, including making her wedding dress and all her attendants' dresses as well then when she is ready. The bride and the bride's party would constantly wear the wedding clothing, keep the lamp full of oil, and keep the wicks trimmed. They did *everything* including sleeping at night in their wedding attire so that they would be ready when the husband returned.

- The next chapter talks about His return and Him taking the bride up and away to the Father's house.
- The wedding feast of the lamb lasts for seven days and is complete in Revelation 19 right before Jesus comes on a white horse.
- The atonement of the bride of the father (the seven-year tribulation)
  o This is a time of reconciliation for the Jewish nation, a time for them to turn to God and be purified, to become that virgin bride for their groom. This is the nation's redemption.
  o It is clearly prophesized in several of the Old Testament prophets like Daniel, Jeremiah, Ezekiel, Isaiah, and Zechariah.
- The tabernacle of the favorite nation living with God in their promised land on earth.
- The tabernacle of the body of Christ living with God in their promised land in heaven.
- The final redemption of *all* mankind occurs at the end of the millennial. This is when *God finally* has *His entire family together for eternity*.
  o Jeremiah prophesized 625 years before Jesus's birth of the new covenant.

> Behold, the days are coming, says the LORD, when I will make a *new covenant* with the house of Israel and with the house of Judah—not according to the covenant that I made with their fathers in the day that I took them by the hand to lead them out of the land of Egypt, *my covenant which they broke, though I was a husband to them, says the LORD*. But this is the covenant, that I will make with the house of Israel after those days, says the LORD: I will put My law in their minds, and write it on their hearts; and

I will be their God, and they shall be My people. (Jeremiah 31:33; emphasis mine)

- o Notice how obvious God associates *the marriage vows with the new covenant. He says they broke the first covenant even though He was their Husband.*
- o The new covenant is what enables man to be born again in the Spirit and be counted worthy to become adopted sons and daughters of our Father in heaven, which enables us to be sanctified as the body of Christ and become the bride of Jesus. *Hallelujah!*
- *The eternal home in paradise*
  - o For the Jewish nation, this is the physical land in the Abrahamic covenant.
  - o For the body of Christ, it is everlasting life with Him in heaven—or wherever He is.

The Typical Ancient Galilean Wedding

The Betrothal

THE TRIUNE NATURE OF THE BRIDE
BRIDE, CHILD OF GOD, WITNESS TO WEDDING

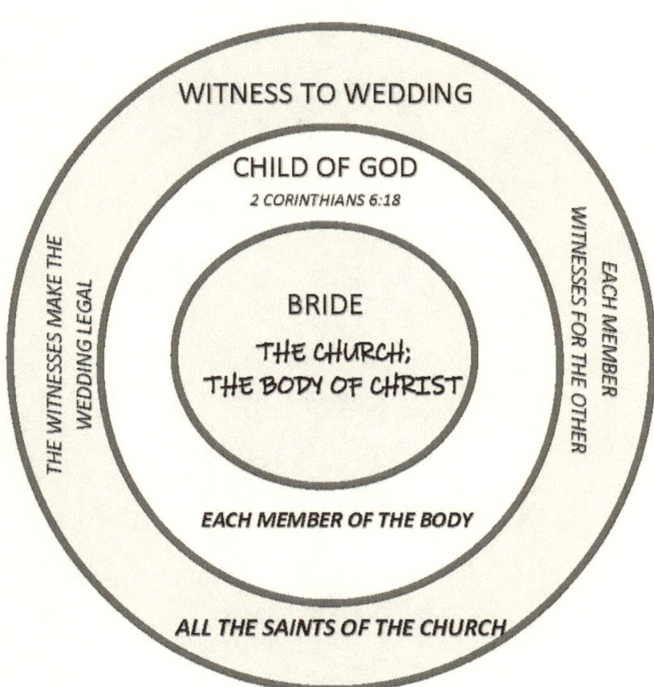

o   Many look at the betrothal as the same as becoming engaged—this is a big mistake.

o   Today being engaged is important to some but is more of a process and one that is easily broken. In the time of Jesus, the betrothed couple were morally and legally married.

> So, her husband, Joseph, being a righteous
> man, and not wanting to disgrace her publicly,
> decided to divorce her secretly. (Matthew 1:19)

In some translations, this is translated as "to put away." The Greek word *apŏluō* means the same, but in this case, divorce is the better translation.

o   Witnesses are extremely important, and the townspeople took this responsibility seriously. In this culture, this was an obligation you had as a neighbor; the whole town would show up.

o   So when it was announced that a betrothal was to occur, by word of mouth, the whole town would hear quickly, and then the bride and groom would meet with all the witnesses present.

o   When they started, they would negotiate the *price of the bride*. There is disagreement on who received this, but I believe it was given to the bride to pay for her living expenses and the cost of preparing for the wedding, while she and her groom would be apart for at least a year.

o   The groom would say his vows to the bride, then he would drink wine from the cup.

o   He would then offer the cup to his bride, and now here is where it was different from other Middle Eastern weddings.

o   The bride could either agree and accept His wedding vows or to reject his offer of marriage. Her rejection would be shown by not doing anything with the cup. If she agreed to proceed with the wedding, she would say her vows of loyalty, trust, and following Him and seal the covenant *by taking and drinking the cup*. They now were in a "common union" with each other. They would not be together to celebrate the wedding feast for some time, so this common union was what they had for *remembrance of each other and of their covenant with each other*. This is the reality of our "common union" (Communion, Appendix B) we (the body of Christ) have with our Lord; *it is* all about *the betrothal*. His Last Supper was truly *the betrothal* between the Groom (Jesus Christ) and His bride (the body of Christ). Like the Galilean betrothal, our betrothal is for remembrance of the Gospel of Jesus Christ, the brokenness He suffered for us, the example He left for us to live, the promise of *His return*, and the *renewal* of our new covenant (our wedding vows), which like the Galilean bride, *we are accepting and renewing our wedding vows every time we drink of the cup*.

o	She would accept His vows and promise to love honor and follow Him all of her days then, once she drank from the cup the *betrothal was completed*. The price of the bride would be paid (see Appendix B). The Galileans said that she was "*being bought with a price*" just as the body of Christ was *bought with a price* the greatest price ever paid! As 1 Corinthians 6:20 states, "*For* you are bought with a price: *therefore, glorify God in your body, and in your spirit, which are God's*." Like the Galilean bride, we are a "purchased possession."

Who is the guarantee of our inheritance until the redemption of the purchased possession, to the praise of His glory. (Ephesians 1:14)

Therefore take heed to yourselves and to all the flock, among which the Holy Spirit has made you overseers, to shepherd the church of God which He purchased with His own blood. (Acts 20:28) o   The groom would tell the bride, "*I now go to my Father's house to build a room for you.*" By Him saying this, his bride knew that he was also *promising her* that he would return to get her and take her to his Father's house.

Jesus promises us the same message:

> Let not your heart be troubled; you believe in God, believe also in Me. In My Father's house are many mansions; if *it were* not *so,* I would have told you. I go to prepare a place for you. And if I go and prepare a place for you, I will come again and receive you to Myself; that where I am, *there* you may be also. And where I go you know, and the way you know. (John 14:1–4)

o   The betrothal was the time for the bride and groom to declare their love for each other, knowing they would soon be apart they needed to express to each other how much love there was between them so that they *would remember* each other for the duration of their separation. Then they would say their vows, their covenant with each other. Their *common union* with each other.

The Year-Long Separation

LONG SEPARATION BRFORE GROOM RETURNS 1 YEAR+	2000+ YEARS FOR JESUS' RETURN
In the Galilean wedding no one knew the day or hour because once all things were prepared the father would decide when *(usually middle of the night)*	**"but of that day and hour no one knows, not even the angels of heaven, but my Father only."** **Matthew 24:36**
Groom would use the time to build onto his father's house	Jesus uses the time to prepare his kingdom for his bride
Bride prepares for the wedding feast – she makes her dress then wears it continually until he comes, she also keeps herself pure, the lamp full of oil and the wick trimmed to be ready for the grooms return	The body of Christ prepares by preparing her dress (the armor of God) then wearing it until he comes, being sanctified (made pure), so the Father can present a glorious bride holy and blameless to his glorious son who is holy/blameless **Ephesians 5:27**
Galilean groom secretly leaves gifts periodically so his bride remembers him, and showing her that he remembers her	Jesus has left his bride *the holy spirit* as a gift and *the ordinance of communion,* to show that he remembers us, and so that we will remember him and the wedding vows
Once ready the Galilean bride and her attendants all keep the candles full of oil, the wicks trimmed and they wear their wedding clothes 24 hours a day to make sure they are ready for the grooms return	In the same way the body of Christ must be constantly ready for Christ's return, by looking for his return *Titus 2:13-14*, living life for him, and wearing the attire he has prepared for us – the armor of god (faith, truth, righteousness, salvation, sword of the spirit, his word) until his return *(we also have to keep our lamps full of oil – the holy spirit)*

Titus 2:13-14 *"looking for the blessed hope and the appearing of our great God And Savior, Christ Jesus, Who gave Himself for us to redeem us from every lawless deed, and to purify for Himself a people for His own possession, zealous for good deeds."*

- The groom would typically be away from his bride with no contact for at least a year. They may be in the same town but would have *no* contact with each other. Therefore, the year-plus separation was hard on both.
- In Jesus's time, the family units were built in a circular fashion to allow additional rooms for many families.
- The groom, even though he would not see his bride, *would leave her gifts* to help her remember him while they were apart.
  - Jesus left us gifts as well:
    - o The gift of the Holy Spirit to comfort and help us while He is away.
    - o The gift of Communion so we can remember Him while He is away from us and so we can remember and renew *His* new *covenant (our wedding vows* with *Him*). This is the real reason for us to frequently have a common union with *Him*— so that we *never forget Him or our covenant (wedding vows) with Him*.
- During that time, the bride was busy preparing for the wedding feast. She would get all material for her gown and the attendants' dresses, then she would make all the dresses and prepare all other necessities for moving into the Father's house. Once she was ready, she and her attendants wore the wedding attire 24-7 and kept the lamp wicks trimmed and full of oil so that they would be ready when the groom returned.
- So many of Christ's parables coincide with the wedding, two of them directly.
  - The wedding of the king's son, this parable is very obvious in its focus on the wedding guests and their total disregard for receiving the invitation.
  - The Jews first, God had sent prophets for hundreds of years with the invitation in hand, but there was always some excuse for not attending.

- We ultimately see many come, but one stands out because they were not dressed appropriately. They came but were not prepared for such a great wedding. In a wedding as great as this one, the King would provide the attire so that all would be prepared. God has given all believers the proper attire; we call it the armor of God. If we are prepared, we come dressed in His shield of faith, His breastplate of righteousness, His belt of truth, we stand ready with the gospel of peace, wearing His helmet of salvation, and carrying His spirit's sword of truth, *His Word*. This is our wedding attire.

- The parable of the ten virgins—it seems like many miss the main point of this wonderful parable.

  o All ten virgins are obviously pure and prepared for the bridegroom to come for them.

  o Five of them were not prepared to wait for the length that was required.

  o The believers who are taken up in the rapture are those that are faithfully watching and expectant for their bridegroom (Jesus) to appear. After all, Jesus taught us, as did the early fathers of the faith, to always be expectant of His return, to always be looking up. His return was to be considered *imminent* by all believers.

  o Had the bridegroom in the parable come at 10:00 p.m., they would have been *all* ready and been taken up together. But you see the bridegroom was delayed, and five of the virgins were distracted and not prepared when he did come.

  o This is exactly why the bride and her attendants in a Galilean wedding would from the time they have all the wedding attire made and are ready for the bridegroom's return will wear the wedding clothes twenty-four hours a day, and keep their lamps full of oil, and the wicks trimmed every day because they are expectant of the return even if it is long overdue, and they are constantly looking for the bridegroom.

o As the bride, we *cannot allow anything to distract us!* The world of Satan and our flesh is constantly trying to distract us. Too many will start focusing on all the problems of the world and will lose their focus on Him or listen to the lies that "it's been two thousand years. Satan's crying out, *he's not coming.*" These are all lies; we need to be faithful and trust in His promised return, and most importantly we need to be like the Galilean bride and wearing our wedding gown twenty-four hours a day, constantly looking up, *expecting Him at any moment. Do not let anything or anyone cause you to take your eyes off Him!*

The Return of the Husband

THE HUSBAND'S RETURN VS. THE RAPTURE

THE HUSBANDS RETURN	THE RAPTURE
The father tells son it is time	The Father in heaven tells Jesus it is time
The son blows the trumpet all the way to the brides house, announcing to the bride and all witnesses that he is coming, 'the last trump is sounded' as he arrives	Jesus blows the trumpet all the way to the brides house, announcing to the bride and all witnesses that he is coming, 'the last trump is sounded' as he arrives
The bride is ready wearing her wedding dress and waiting	The Body of Christ is ready wearing her wedding dress (armor of God) and waiting
The bride is put into a litter and lifted and taken up to the father's house	The body of Christ is taken up to the Father's house

- One thing that was very different in the Galilean wedding was that no one knew the time of the wedding feast except the father. This is because the father would wait until he knew all preparations were done, then when even the son did not expect, the father would randomly wake up in the middle of the night, and if no one had inquired about when it was going to be for a while, he would then surprise his son by waking him and telling him, "The time is now." This is the same we hear Jesus describing in Matthew 24:36–51, where He says even the angels don't know the time.

- As soon as the father tells the son the time is now, he picks up the shofar and blows it. Then he and his father walk down the street to the bride's house, all the way blowing the trumpet (shofar).
- The blowing of the trumpet wakes the residents of the town who come out and follow the father and the groom as the witnesses—again this is a special obligation that they took very seriously—and this time there would be food!
- Scriptures in the New Testament about His return for the bride:

Taking up of the Tribulation Saint

And He will send His angels with a great sound of a trumpet, and they will gather together His elect from the four winds, from one end of heaven to the other. (Matthew 24:31)

Taking up of the Bride of Christ

In a moment, in the twinkling of an eye, at the last trumpet. For the trumpet will sound, and the dead will be raised incorruptible, and we shall be changed. (1 Corinthians 15:52)

For the Lord Himself will descend from heaven with a shout, with the voice of an archan-

gel, and with the trumpet of God. And the dead
in Christ will rise first. (1 Thessalonians 4:16)

- o   The sound of the trumpet in the above verses has
  caused confusion among theologians for two mil-
  lennia; most all have come to the conclusion that it
  is referring to the last trumpet of Revelation. I was
  always confused because the Jews at the time Jesus
  and the disciples were teaching did not have the book
  of Revelation to refer to; in fact, it would be close to
  thirty years before John would reveal his vision.
- o   The blowing of the trumpet was common in the
  Jewish world.
- It was common for the trumpet to be sounded at the beginning and at the end of all important events, with the end
  trump being called the *last trump*.
  - o   In Thessalonians 4:16, it is the Lord Himself with the
    trumpet, and in Revelation, it is the angel.
  - o   In 1 Corinthians 15:52, the "last trumpet" in this
    verse is the one that causes a lot of confusion. When
    I heard the words, "It's all about the wedding," this
    verse just came alive, *of course, the wedding.*

GALILEAN WEDDING VS. JESUS' PROMISE

THE BETROTHAL	LONG SEPARATION	HUSBAND'S RETURN	THE WEDDING FEAST
BRIDE BOUGHT WITH A PRICE	THE LONG SEPARATION	GALILEAN WEDDING	IN THE FATHER'S HOUSE
TIME OF REMEMBRANCE BEFORE LONG SEPARATION	1 YEAR PLUS FOR GALILEAN WEDDING	THE FATHER TELLS SON IT'S TIME ALL THE WAY TO THE BRIDES HOUSE, THE SON BLOWS THE TRUMPET WITH SHOUTS OF JOY	7 DAYS FOR THE GALILEAN WEDDING
GROOM SAYS VOWS	THE GIFT OF REMEMBRANCE	*AS THE LAST TRUMP SOUNDS* THEY ARRIVE AT THE BRIDE'S HOUSE TO TAKE HER UP AND AWAY TO THE FATHERS HOUSE..	7 YEARS FOR THE BODY OF CHRIST
BRIDE ACCEPTS GROOMS VOWS BY	GALILEAN GROOM SECRETLY LEAVES GIFTS		BASED ON DANIEL'S SEVENTY WEEKS
ACCEPTING THE CUP	JESUS LEAVES		
DRINKING THE WINE	THE HOLY SPIRIT		
BRIDE'S VOW TO LOVE, OBEY, AND FOLLOW GROOM	COMMUNION	RAPTURE - THE LORD HIMSELF WILL DESCEND FROM HEAVEN WITH A SHOUT, WITH THE VOICE OF AN ARCHANGEL, AND WITH THE TRUMPET OF GOD. AND THE DEAD IN CHRIST WILL RISE FIRST. 1 THES 4:16	DURING THE 7 YEAR TRIBULATION
GROOMS PROMISE TO RETURN NO MATTER HOW LONG	"BUT OF THAT DAY AND HOUR NO ONE KNOWS, NOT EVEN THE ANGELS OF HEAVEN, BUT MY FATHER ONLY."		THE TIME OF JACOB'S TROUBLE
"I GO TO PREPARE A ROOM FOR YOU AT MY FATHER'S HOUSE"			THE JEWS ATTONEMENT

JESUS' LAST SUPPER (COMMON-UNION) COMMUNION	>2000 YEARS FOR JESUS' RETURN	THE RAPTURE	THE WEDDING FEAST

- When the Father determined that the time was right for the wedding feast, He gave the shofar to the Groom (Jesus), who blew it starting at His Father's house all the way through town to give notice to all the witnesses, right up to the point where He stops at the bride's house with the last trumpet sound.
- As he was arriving at the bride's house, he would *blow the last trumpet, and at that sound,* he would have arrived to pick up his bride to lift her up and take her away.
- When he arrived at the house, the bride and her attendants would be waiting. The groom would have a "litter" that the bride would be placed into, and two men would take her "*up and away to the Father's house.*" Some call this the "flight to the Father's house."

The Wedding Feast

THE WEDDING FEAST ON EARTH VS. IN HEAVEN

EARTHLY WEDDING FEAST	HEAVENLY WEDDING FEAST
In the father's house	In the Father's house
Bride and guests all arrive and doors are closed	Bride and guests all arrive and doors are closed
Feast lasts for 7 days	Feast lasts for 7 days (years) Based on Daniel's 70 week of years
During the feast – the greatest celebration in the bride and groom's lives	During the celebration in heaven the greatest celebration in all of mankind
During the wedding celebration the witnesses and others who were invited, who were not ready and did not make it are sorrowful because it was their obligation to be witnesses	During the wedding celebration the people on earth are experiencing 7 years of the tribulation Jacob's trouble and the Jews atonement
After the ceremony the bride is dressed in her new clothes and she follows her groom to claim the wonderful life waiting them	After the wedding the bride is arrayed in a white robe clean and bright (revelation 19:8) then she follows the groom on the white horse to claim His kingdom and eliminate evil
The bride and groom are now a family on earth	We are now a family of God in heaven, with Jesus as our husband, we are a child of God the Father, and we have brothers and sisters like never before

o   All the townspeople have come out and followed the groom to be witnesses (extremely critical).

o   They enter, and as soon as the last goes into the house, the doors are closed and locked, and anyone late is locked out and not allowed entry to the doors that would be locked! We cannot be late for the rapture!

o   The Galilean wedding feast lasts for seven days.

Throughout *Jesus's ministry*, He used terms and phrases that His disciples who were all Galilean would immediately be able to associate with the wedding and know precisely the message Jesus was giving them without Him having to explain it. This is why many of the secrets in scripture would not be known until the last days; when we apply the knowledge of the Galilean wedding to our readings, we see many things that were before hidden.

-   I go to prepare a room for you in my Father's house—It was His promise to return to get them and take them to the marriage feast.

    This also answers many questions that theologians have argued about for two millennia.

-   The trumpet or last trumpet is not the seventh trumpet in Revelation. That is the last trumpet before the wrath *as virtually every theologian believes*, but they all have failed to understand or remember the Galilean wedding and how much it is used throughout the entire Bible. It is the last trumpet blown as Jesus arrives for His bride when no one is expecting, the Father will tell Jesus, "Now is the time. Go gather your bride." He will come with the sound of the trumpet blowing the entire way to us and at His last trumpet sound, He will have arrived. Those who are ready will be taken away (flown away) just like the bride in the ancient Galilean wedding—to the Father's house, and anyone late in coming will be left gnashing their teeth and weeping trying to get in, but they were not ready (Matthew 24:31; 1 Corinthians 15:52; 1 Thessalonians 4:16; Mark 13:27).

- God has provided to us His appointment book with the important dates on the calendar, showing us the appointed times for the major events that Jesus will perform for the atonement of His favorite nation and the redemption of all mankind. He has asked all of us to remember each of these appointments until He comes again. (Appendix C)

The wedding feast lasts for seven days.

Revelation chapter 19 describes the wedding supper and in verses 6–8,

> And I heard, as it were, the voice of a great multitude, as the sound of many waters and as the sound of mighty thundering, saying, Alleluia! For the Lord God Omnipotent reigns! Let us be glad and rejoice and give Him glory, for the marriage of the Lamb has come, and His wife has made herself ready. And to her it was granted to be *arrayed in fine linen, clean and bright*, for the fine linen is the righteous acts of the saints. (Emphasis mine)

This is the end of the wedding supper, which most who understand the Jewish culture believe would have to last seven days, and many when taking all the other things into consideration believe the wedding supper starts at the beginning of the seven-year tribulation and then ends in Revelation 19:14, "And the armies in heaven, clothed in fine linen, white and clean, followed Him on white horse." Jesus is followed by His bride, whom He granted to be arrayed in the fine linen, clean and bright. Hallelujah.

The seven-year tribulation is another book, but I will stir the pot a little more and tell you that there is no question in my mind that the entire seven-year tribulation is for the "anointing of the Jews."

Another divine secret is in Matthew 24:37, "But as the days of Noah were, so also will the coming of the Son of Man be." In the days of Noah, the people had all forgotten about God and His moral laws;

they had become apostates. Then God called Noah to build the ark to rescue all the righteous and the animals. This was the physical before the spiritual. There was one door in the ark through which everyone had to enter. In the last days, Jesus is the one and only door, the way into the ark. All are called into the ark, but most ridicule Noah and the ark. Today Jesus is being ridiculed, and Romans chapter 1 is being played out right in front of all of us. After inviting the people to repent and turn their lives around, no one came except eight people. Many are called, but few are chosen. The door is closed, and once it is closed, no one else can enter. In the Galilean wedding, all the guests are invited, but if they do not get there in time, the door will close, and they will not be welcomed. This is the same with the rapture; all are invited, but few will choose to follow Jesus. Once Jesus comes, at the last trump to pick up His bride and take her up to His Father's house, the door is closed, and the wedding feast will have begun. And just like in the days of Noah, or like the five virgins who ran out of oil, they will *all* miss the wedding feast because they did not listen and follow Jesus.

THE GREAT MYSTERY OF THE MARRIAGE

For we are members of His body, of His flesh and of His bones. "For this reason a man shall leave his father and mother and be joined to his wife, and the two shall become one flesh." This is a great mystery, but I speak concerning Christ and the church

THE MODEL GODLY MARRIAGE ON EARTH

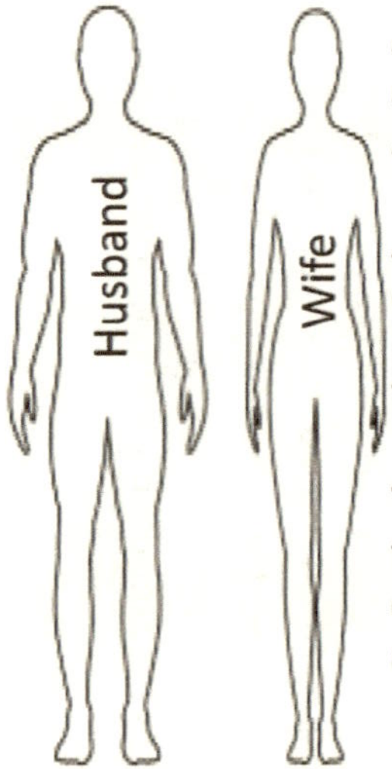

Husband

Wife

And Adam said: "This *is now bone of my bones*
And flesh of my flesh;

As Husband and Wife a married couple *becomes* "AS ONE FLESH"

The Husband is the head

The Wife was made to be closer to the husband than anything else could ever be, they were made to be as close to one as physically possible

THE REAL GODLY MARRIAGE IN HEAVEN

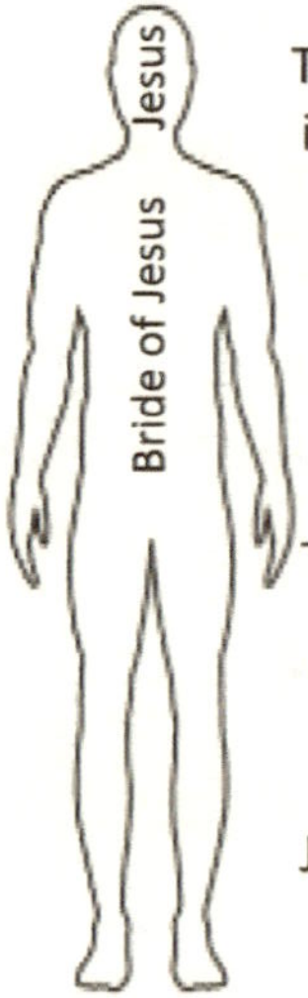

Jesus

Bride of Jesus

The great mystery of the marriage is When Jesus was describing the relationship between Husband and Wife on the Earth, He was describing the Perfect union between Himself and His Bride the Church

The earthly marriage could never be completely one as God designed because they had two physical bodies

Jesus fixed that by putting us (His Bride) into His Spiritual Body

There is one more divine secret we must reveal before leaving this book about the wedding.

> For we are members of His body, of His
> flesh and of His bones, "For this reason a man
> shall leave his father and mother and be joined
> to his wife, and the two shall become one flesh."
> This is a great mystery, but I speak concerning
> Christ and the church. (Ephesians 5:30–32)

The whole time Jesus was talking about the responsibilities of the husband, bride, and children in Ephesians chapter 5, he was revealing a huge divine secret. The entire time Jesus was describing the marriage between Him and the church. Some referred to this as a type and antitype; look closely at what he is saying. He started, "We are members of His body, His flesh, His bones." Remember the physical always comes first, then the spiritual. And again we can tell the end from the beginning. Eve was the first bride, and God did not create her out of clay; she was created from Adam's body. There was no way to create her so that she would be closer to him than to be made out of his flesh. This was all natural, and now Jesus is showing us through Paul that the body of Christ, His bride, is made out of His (Christ's) flesh and His bones. This is the spiritual state of the last bride, the one who has become "the body of Christ," the fullness of Jesus Christ as Ephesians 1:23 says, "Which is His body, the fullness of Him who fills all in all." This is why it's so important that the body be sanctified to be presented to the Groom spotless and without blemish.

We are truly bone of His bone and flesh of His flesh; we have His DNA in our bodies *right now*. We have His blood flowing through our veins *right now*. When we truly grasp this, believe it with our whole being, then we will be transformed in a way that we cannot even imagine. We have the authority, the glory, the grace, and the love that we need to have *all* things that we ask for in *His name*, so let's start using them. He then continues that a man shall leave his father and mother. Jesus left His Father in heaven so that He could come down to earth and join His wife the church and become *one flesh* with her. This helps explain His response, if you remember when His parents found Him in the temple. They were anxious and full of fear. But as Luke 2:49 says, And He said to them, "Why did you seek Me? Did you not know that I must be about My Father's business?" You see, He had already started to separate Himself from His earthly parents to become one flesh with His bride. His whole life was focused on becoming *one* with *His body*. This is why it is so very important that we abide in Him and He in us. John chapter 15 explains that we must be one flesh, only He provides examples like the vine and the branches, indicating that the vine provides the life-giving blood to us. Think of that, when we are truly *abiding in Him*, we have *His* DNA, *His blood*, flowing through our veins. Wow! He goes on to tell us that we can't produce fruit if we don't abide in Him. Then in 2 John 1:9, "Anyone who goes too far and does not abide in the teaching of Christ, does not have God; the one who abides in the teaching, he has both the Father and the Son."

If we truly are abiding *in Him*, we not only have *Him*, but we also have the *Father*. Brothers and sisters, we could continue with more verses that show the mystery, but I hope by now you are convinced as I was at 2:00 a.m. when I received the divine secret that Jesus's whole life on earth, including *His death* and *resurrection*, was all for the *wedding*. He defeated sin and death so that we can abide in Him and He in us. His teachings were all to provide us with the wisdom and knowledge to understand His great grace, giving us justification (the key that opens the gate to the narrow path) by grace through faith (Ephesians 2:2–10) and then teaching us about the narrow path that is hard and few will take—the path to sanctification through the Holy Spirit (2 Thessalonians 2:13), our purification through the refiner's fire, and then our final victory when we reach the end of the narrow path and receive our new glorious bodies that are taken up to the Father's house for the wedding feast. Oh, what a *great divine secret*. Hallelujah! Hallelujah! Hallelujah!

WORDS IN SCRIPTURE THAT BRING REMEMBRANCE OF THE BRIDE

The bride is the Fullness of the groom who Fills all in all *Ephesians 1:22*

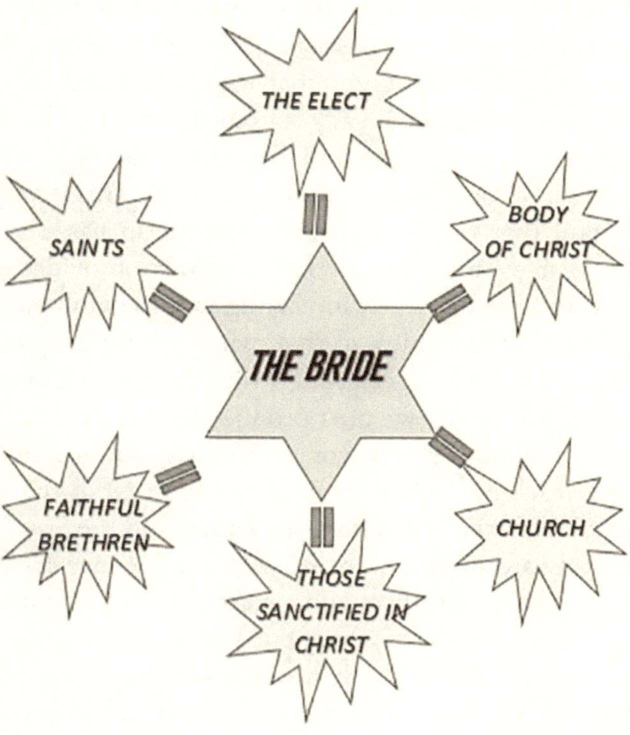

God wants the bride as a <u>glorious church</u> holy & without blemish because <u>the groom</u> is holy and without blemish Ephesians 5:27

Remember when you abide in the Word that *all* God has ever wanted is a true family, so look for the wedding, look for all the glory of the wedding. Remember His promises and the true *end price* awaiting His bride. Look for the word *covenant* anywhere in the Bible and associate it with the wedding wows, either the Abrahamic with God the Father or the new covenant with Jesus. When you see the words *church, body of Christ, saints, faithful brethren,* those who are sanctified in Christ Jesus, remember the bride, you and me, and His coming to take us up to His Father's house for the marriage feast.

Every time you see a passage concerning our sanctification, or you see He wants to present us as a chaste virgin, or as pure and holy, or as a glorious church without spot or wrinkle, remember we are His bride, and He is holy, pure, without spot or wrinkle. We are both His bride and His body, which means that if we are anything less, then He would be "unevenly yoked with His ride" and in constant conflict with His body, which God would *never* allow, thus, the reason for our sanctification (purification) in the fire of the Holy Spirit. Also, every time you celebrate Communion with Him, *always* remember the reason for this *amazing* celebration. It's a time of remembrance. Like the Galilean groom, Jesus knew He would be gone for an extended time, so He provides us a time to remember Him and keep Him close to our hearts. It is also a time of *renewal,* a recommitment of our wedding vows, to ensure our readiness for His return. Thank you again for reading about the revealing of the divine mysteries I had at 2:00 a.m. I pray they impact your abiding in Christ as much as they have mine.

The final appointment in God's appointment book (again something that will require a much larger narrative) is the establishment of the millennial kingdom, the Feast of Tabernacles, when man again will tabernacle with God as He did with Adam and Eve. This happens right after Jesus and His bride (you and me) return to rebuke Satan and evil from this present world. There are many more mysteries and divine secrets in God's remaining appointments. I hope to share those with you soon. Hallelujah and Amen. God's blessings to all who read this. I love you all!

THE FAMILY OF GOD

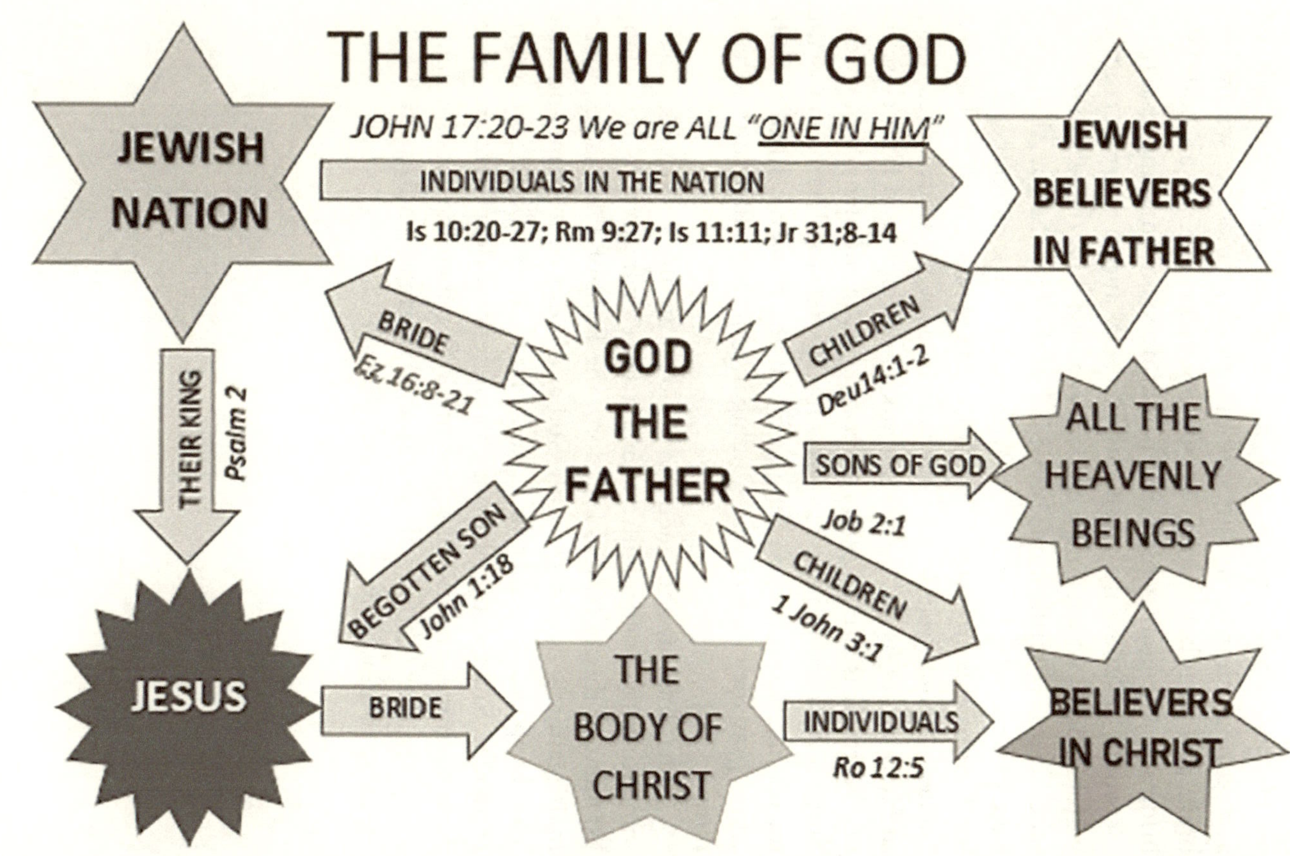

Appendix A

The Family of God

This topic probably should have its own little mini-book because there is so much to cover.

We are all God's children, and we are all the brides of Christ, but there is so much more to the family of God.

He created us to be *His family*. So He gave us a structure similar to the structure He has in heaven. Just like His structure in heaven, there are different dimensions of God's family. We have a Triune Godhead: the Father, Son, and Holy Ghost; but under that Godhead is another triune, *"the heavenly family triune."* This triune can be confusing like the Godhead. It consists of the husband, the wife, and the children. Some ask how can this be confusing. Too many always try to figure out how God can be three different persons in one God. It is the same with the family.

Let's start with the children of God. Each of us is a child of God. All together as a unified group, we are the bride, and when we abide in Him completely and He abides in us we *become one in Him*, just like the *Godhead*.

He created a family triune here on earth to represent His family triune in heaven. We have an earthly husband who is the head of the family, the wife (bride) who cares for the family, and the children.

This is why one of the original commandments was to honor your mother and father; it was a command to prepare us for our *real life* with Him.

As a side note, I was always a little confused about whom the witnesses at the wedding feasts described in Scripture. We notice that if they are late, the doors are locked, and they will never enter and be left outside wailing and gnashing their teeth. I believe that the *bride* as a unified unit is inside, but we as individuals are the wedding guests, and many will not come to believe until it is too late and they will be screaming to get in, but the wedding feast has begun, and they are too late.

Appendix B

The evening before Jesus was slain on the cross, He and His disciples had what we call the Last Supper. Jesus tells us in Luke 22:15–16, "Then He said to them, With fervent desire I have desired to eat this Passover with you before I suffer; for I say to you, I will no longer eat of it *until it is fulfilled* in the kingdom of God." It will be fulfilled with the rapture, and He will eat again at the wedding feast.

The wedding started with the betrothal and is represented by the first "common union" (what we refer to as Communion) between Jesus and His bride, "the body of Christ." This is a divine secret that became obvious to the disciples after the resurrection when they remembered what He had said and done. This is when they realized that Jesus used the Galilean wedding as a model; it was then that all the pieces came together, and they could see how Jesus had planned everything He did for the ultimate perfect ending, when they would meet Him in the sky and go to His Father's house, where He had prepared a room for them and have the wedding feast.

Paul initially reprimands the Corinthians in 1 Corinthians chapter 11:17–33: *He wanted to commend them* but he couldn't when it came to observing the Last Supper. Their conduct during the sacred event was deplorable, outrageous, and immoral—it was sinful in the greatest sense. They were making a mockery of God's ordinance and required a sharp rebuke.

The ordinances of Christ are intended to be a blessing to the believer, to promote good spiritual health and be a reminder to help them live a godly life and imitate Jesus. Paul was frustrated because through their carnality, they had turned the ordinance into an apostate ceremony, which in turn *became a curse to them rather than a blessing*. He said there are many who are weak and sick as a result.

Paul then rebukes them for attempting to legitimize their conduct by inviting someone who appears *genuine* (someone others recognize as being pure and walking in the Spirit, probably someone respected by the church). The Companion Bible shows that verse 29 in the *original manuscripts* reads, "For he that eateth and drinketh, eateth and drinketh damnation to himself *since he does not discern the body." They were bringing nonbelievers into the celebration of the body, not recognizing* the "common membership" of the body of Christ. They were being disrespectful of the body of Christ. This all goes back to the wedding; the saints are all part of the body of Christ, the bride of Christ. When we come into a "common union," we must humble ourselves and be one; we must seek to *be one* in the Spirit of Jesus Christ. The eating of the bread is the bride's time to remember *during the long separation* of a year or more, the Groom for who He is, what He has done, and His promise to return for her, and the drinking of the wine is the bride's renewal of the wedding vows, the new covenant. If we refuse to eat or drink, or if we eat and drink in an improper manner, not as one in the Spirit with Jesus Christ, we are just like the bride who rejects the Groom's covenant (vows), and we are condemned.

When we treat this the way Jesus intended, as the betrothal, then we realize that we are the bride, and we understand that every time we celebrate this ordinance, we are celebrating a time of "the betrothal" between Jesus and His bride—*you* and *me.* As often as we do it, we do it in *remembrance and renewal*—remembrance with the bread before the supper and renewal of our vows as supper ended.

- Before dinner, He took the bread, blessed it, and broke it and said, "This is My body which is given for you; do this in remembrance of Me."
  - o When a couple would come together for their betrothal, it was a great celebration. The entire town would be involved as witnesses for such an important occasion. The fathers would negotiate the bride's price, which was given to the bride's parents from the groom's parents. Some believe that in the Galilean cer-

emony, the price is given to the bride so she had the money she needed to pay for the things she required to prepare for the wedding, for the next year, while her husband was away taking care of building an extra room onto his father's house. In either case, because of the money changing hands, she was thought of as *"being bought with a price."*

For you were bought at a price; therefore, glorify God in your body and in your spirit, which is God's. (1 Corinthians 6:20)

o *Just like the Galilean bride, we are being asked to remember our Groom while He is away from us.*
o We are to remember *His broken body on the cross and that He gave his life for us!*
o Just like a bride waiting for her husband to come home from an extended stay, away from her (the Galilean Groom would be away for a year or more), we are to remember these:
  - How much we love Him.
  - His life and how much He means to us.
  - The things that are so special about Him.
    - His humility.
    - His gentleness, kindness, compassion, empathy, mercy, grace, and agape.
    - The joy He fills us with.
  - His suffering, death, burial, and resurrection.
  - His ascension (John 14:2–6).
  - His promise of our ascension. The Galilean bride was awaiting the groom's return so she could be put into a "liter" and "taken up and away to the Father's house" to live with the groom.
  - His whole life.

- The example He left for us to follow.

  The example so that we can live our life *for Him* and become His image so that when we look in the mirror, we see his glory (Corinthians 3:18). We then become the image for others to follow, which is what God had planned from the beginning.
- His lessons on life and how to treat others.

  He wants us to remember that just like the Galilean bride, we were *bought* with a *price*—a great invaluable price in His life.

Most importantly we are to remember

- o to love Him with our heart, mind, soul, and strength and
- o to love our neighbor as ourselves.

- After dinner, He took the cup and said, "Take this and drink it, this cup *is* the new covenant in My blood, which is shed for you." Blood was used for two purposes: the atonement of sins and the agreement and sealing of a new covenant.
  - o Jesus is talking about His new covenant with His bride—the wedding vows for the body of Christ.
- *Intimacy*—Before this, the people had to wait once a year for their atonement, and then it was through a third party (the high priest) Jesus *tore the curtain of the sanctuary down*, and now we have access *directly to Him* anytime we desire.
- *Oneness with Him*—We are one with *Him* just as *He* is *one* with the *Father* (John 17:21).
- We have *His laws* and *commandments in our hearts*—This is the new covenant that Jeremiah 31:33 prophesized, where God would put the Law in their minds and write it on their hearts.

- *A helper and comforter Holy Spirit.* While on earth, Jesus set His glory aside so that He could experience the same pain, emotions, and temptations as a man and provide us an example of how to live in the evil world by relying on the Holy Spirit. Consequently, He left us the same helper and comforter He had when He set aside His glory.
- *Power*—Our helper and comforter gives us gifts, *His fruit*, and *power* to glorify our *Lord God* in all *things*.

Then just as in the Galilean betrothal, after each one repeats the vows, the Groom offers the bride the cup of wine. She has the choice of whether to accept or reject the wedding vows. By taking a drink from the cup, we are accepting the covenant—the wedding vows, committing to surrender all to Him, submit to Him, obey Him, follow Him, and serve Him through eternity.

Our vow to Him is to surrender all to Him, trust Him, and follow Him with *agape love forever*.

We are now married to Christ, awaiting the wedding feast!

Appendix C

His calendar contains seven appointments that represent the major events or milestones in His plan for the redemption of the world; we are to keep all of them yearly. Each one includes a physical fulfilling and a spiritual fulfilling as follows:

Appointment	Physical Fulfilling	Spiritual Fulfilling
Passover	The Passover lambs' blood saved Israelites in Egypt.	Jesus's blood saves the body of Christ.
Feast of Unleavened Bread	The Jews deliverance out of Egypt's houses swept of all leaven (sin and evil).	Jesus has victory over sin and evil in the grave.
Feast of First Fruits	The first fruits of the spring season are offered as a sacrifice.	Jesus is resurrected to become the first fruit of the dead.
Feast of Weeks	Moses delivers the Law to the Israelites.	The Holy Spirit is delivered to the body of Christ, Pentecost.
Feast of Trumpets	Rosh Hashanah is a new year a new beginning.	Not fulfilled yet—we expect a new year and a new beginning to be taken up with him.
Feast of Atonement	When there was a temple, the Jews celebrated the Feast of Atonement every year through sacrifice— the blood of one would be sprinkled on the altar while	The tribulation is the seven years that Daniel talked about, calling it Jacob's trouble. Ezekiel and others have prophesized in detail the troubled times that the Jews must endure for their atonement, which is why the tribulation is known in many
	another was let go as a scapegoat—today they celebrate by spending the entire day in prayer and meditation.	circles as the atonement of the Jews.
Feast of Tabernacles	The Jews celebrate this every year as a remembrance of the forty years when they tabernacled with God in the desert.	The spiritual fulfillment will come when Jesus sets up His millennial kingdom on earth and the Jews again will tabernacle with the Lord for one thousand years.

There are other dates God has set aside on his calendar, and they all involve the perfect completion number of seven:

- The seventh day is the Sabbath of days.
- The seventh year is the Sabbath of years (the shemittah).
- The year after the seventh shemittah is the Sabbath of Jubilees.

Each one is very special in God's eyes and requires a separate document focused strictly on the Sabbaths.

During our study of the Word, it is very useful to keep track of the shemittahs and the Jubilees.

Ten consecutive shemittahs is seventy years, which is the perfect spiritual completion with the number 7 and the hand of God the number 10. Put together, it is the perfect wholeness or oneness in God.

About the Author

The author, Dr. Joseph A. Herr, started life on his family dairy farm, close to God's wonderful creation. Upon graduation, with the computer revolution just starting, he decided to forego a football scholarship and started helping businesses find and resolve their business issues.

He knew how important education was, so for seventeen years, he worked full-time and went to school to attain both his bachelor of science in business administration and master of business administration.

All this time God was calling him into the ministry, but he just kept unknowingly running away. God gave him a very successful career. He was an international speaker and author of risk and improvement articles in local publications. After about thirty years, God finally got ahold of him and guided him to take some seminary courses. He found that while he was helping businesses uncover the rocks that would sink their ship, he could do the same thing for God, but this time he would be helping others *find* the only rock that would keep their ship afloat—Jesus. God showed him that just as Jesus prophesized, the church was becoming the enemy within and accepting the world and man's doctrine rather than God's. He showed him He needs more warriors to find and illuminate the *truth* that has been lost and to find the mysteries that God has hidden, which are to be revealed in the end days.

He has accepted the calling and has been searching with urgency ever since. He finds that every time he reads a scripture, He shows him something new and wonderful. He loves to find the Jewish cultural settings and the language used at the time of Jesus. This allows him to relate to scripture in a great new way—a way that is more intimate and makes everything come alive before his eyes. He finds that the Bible is full of these kinds of things.

Nothing in his writing is from him though—he is not that smart; it is truly from God. Dr. Herr has honestly been shown sermons where he asked, "Where did this come from? This is awesome," only to find it was him who said it. The words came out of his mouth, but they originated *in Him*. Praise God.